Matt and Kyle's proven commit
small communities has been evi
helpful insight and practical ways to keep the gospel above all in
many of America's forgotten places.

> **Dr. J.D. Greear.** *Pastor of The Summit Church, Raleigh, North Carolina; President of the Southern Baptist Convention*

In *Replanting Rural Churches* Matt Henslee and Kyle Bueermann write from an ink well of sound theology and practical experience. Scripture flows in their bloodstream and rural dirt is caked between their toes, they have been there, they are there, and they are loving their ministries. There are many things to love about this book, but, for one, I am thankful that they offered no clever schemes for church reclamation, but looked instead to the Bible. Wherever you are in ministry, Madison Avenue or Dry Pond Road, you will be encouraged and instructed from this book. And, Matt and Kyle write conversationally and with just the right touch of humor. Most of all, Matt and Kyle are men of God who want to glorify Him as they declare His truth and minister to His people. I delightfully commend this work to you.

> **Ray Rhodes, Jr.** *Author of* Susie: The Life and Legacy of Susannah Spurgeon *(Moody), and pastor of four SBC churches over three decades.*

Replanting Rural Churches is not just another Baptist book on pastoral ministry. Pastors Matt Henslee and Kyle Bueermann call upon the called to reconsider and to reimagine the possibilities of ministering to churches in rural contexts. *Replanting Rural Churches'* rural revitalization ministry principles of preaching, praying, passion, and perseverance will encourage pastors and ministers who live and serve in rural communities, as well as challenge would-be pastors and ministers to consider doing ministry in rural churches. Having served as a pastor in a rural context, I heartily recommend this book!

> **Matt Queen,** *Associate Professor and L. R. Scarborough Chair of Evangelism ("The Chair of Fire"); Associate Director of Doctoral Programs; Southwestern Baptist Theological Seminary, Fort Worth, Texas*

As a pastor of a church located between Milksick Cove and Hooker's Gap, just east of Jugtown, I was much interested in this book. We are not at the end of the world, but you can see it out the back door. Can I get a witness? I cannot tell you how many times I have felt like the red-headed step-child with a ministry as insignificant as an ice cube sitting on the polar cap. Matt Henslee and Kyle Bueermann essentially shout, "Put on your big boy pants, get over yourself, roll up your sleeves and get to work!" This is such an encouraging book for every pastor and people whose theme song is the Beatles' "Nowhere Man." You matter. You matter to God. Matt and Kyle do more than just encourage rural ministries— important as that is. They give practical help for such congregations to make a significant impact for the Kingdom that far exceeds their attendance and location. Read this. Apply it. Buy some copies and send it to some friends—even if by pony express or carrier pigeon!

Dennis Thurman, *Senior Pastor, Pole Creek Baptist Church, Candler, NC*

The small rural church is more common than the mega urban church, but it seems like mega urban churches have all the fun and get all the attention. In *Replanting Rural Churches*, Matt and Kyle offer an honest and transparent appraisal of rural ministry as well as an encouraging message for those serving in a rural context. This book is theologically insightful and practically resourceful. I cannot recommend X enough to anyone pastoring in a rural setting, or in any setting for that matter!

Dr. Jared Wellman, *Lead Pastor, Tate Springs*

Replanting Rural Churches is a fun, personal, and practical testimony about being a pastor. Matt and Kyle offer hope, encouragement, and action steps that guide us toward faithful ministry. Whether you are in a joyful or dry season of leadership, this book serves as a witty and winsome guide for those who lead churches.

Dr. Philip Nation, *Director of Global Impact Churches for the Baptist World Alliance and author of* Habits for Our Holiness

REPLANTING
RURAL CHURCHES

Available in the Replant Series

Am I a Replanter?: 30 Days of Discerning God's Call, Bob Bickford &
Mark Hallock

Be a Barnabas: Helping Your Replant Be All God Wants It to Be, Mark
Hallock

*God's Not Done with Your Church: Finding Hope and New Life through
Replanting,* Mark Hallock

*Pathways to Partnership: How You and Your Church Can Join the
Replanting Movement,* Bob Bickford & Mark Hallock

Raising Up Replanters: A Start-Up Guide for Your Church,
Mark Hallock

Replant 101: How You Can Help Revitalize Dying Churches,
Mark Hallock

*Replant Roadmap: How Your Congregation Can Help Revitalize Dying
Churches,* Mark Hallock

*Replanting Rural Churches: God's Plan and Call for the Middle of
Nowhere,* Matt Henslee & Kyle Bueermann

REPLANTING RURAL CHURCHES

God's plan and call for the middle of nowhere

Matt Henslee & Kyle Bueermann

Foreword by Mark Clifton

Matt —
Dedicated to the love of my life, Rebecca, our four amazing daughters, and an awesome church in the middle of nowhere, Mayhill Baptist Church.

Kyle —
Dedicated to my amazing wife Michelle, and our incredible kids Noah and Hailey. I'm glad you're the people I get to share life with!

CONTENTS

FOREWORD

Can anything good come out of Nazareth?

Nathaniel asked that question of Phillip in the first chapter of John's Gospel. I love Philip's answer. He simply said, "Come and see."

Nathaniel's question was understandable. Nazareth was not exactly the center of the universe. In fact, it wasn't the center of anything. It was a small, out of the way, insignificant village of less than a thousand people. In many ways, Nazareth is not unlike countless numbers of villages, communities, crossroads, and towns across North America today.

For most people who live in the cities and urban centers of this continent, these little, out-of-the-way rural places have no significance. They don't impact the culture. With cities growing so rapidly, they don't seem to be strategically important either.

But you and I know, nothing could be further from the truth. Every village, community, crossroad, and town in North America is a location where people need to hear the gospel. Every person in those communities is a person whom Jesus loves, and he died for.

Jesus died for the people in Spickard, Mo. There may be only 487 people in the town. You won't find a Walmart there. You won't find a grocery store. You won't even find a gas station.

Unfortunately, today you won't find a church either. My dad was born in that town 90-plus years ago. A little more than 70 years ago, the town's First Baptist Church was my dad's first pastorate. He preached his first-ever Easter sermon there in 1947. He met my mom for the first time there. That church is where they married.

But today, that church no longer exists. About a year and a half ago, I received a call from the local Baptist association saying they were closing it down. They asked whether I wanted to keep any of my dad's stuff that had been left there. It's about two hours away from where I live in Kansas, so I drove up there and spent a day in Spickard.

As I prayed over the community that day, I grieved. I love that town. More importantly, Jesus does too. But today the community has a limited gospel witness.

Spickard may not have a Walmart, a grocery store, or a gas station, but it has a school. Thirty-seven percent of that town is under the age of 15. That means a generation of children are growing up without an opportunity to hear about Jesus through a gospel-preaching church.

Many people may look at towns like Spickard as simply fly-over or drive-by country. You and I know different. We know that God is at work in every home, on every farm, in every ranch, and in every community. As our friend Henry Blackaby has reminded us in Experiencing God, we need to find out where God is at work and join him in it.

That's why I believe this Replanting Rural Churches is a wonderful treasure for the church. The book helps us understand where God is at work in rural America and how we can join him in that work. In my role of leading the replant team for the North American Mission Board, I am constantly hearing the question, "Where are the resources for helping rural leaders revitalize their churches in North America?" The book in your hand is the answer. It is written by two men who are doing just that under the leadership of the Holy Spirit. In the book, they share with us what God has been teaching them—and our rural churches will be better because of what they are teaching.

I highly recommend this book. I believe God can and will work in amazing ways through men and women who are willing to make themselves available to be used by him in small towns across North America. As church leaders begin to apply the teaching in this book, I believe we will see God's glory made known once again in every little Nazareth and Spickard on this continent.

I can't wait for that day.

Mark Clifton
Senior Director of Replant
North American Mission Board

ACKNOWLEDGEMENTS

Matt — A special thanks to Southwestern Baptist Theological Seminary and many professors that would be too long to list that taught me to preach the Word and love my people well.

Kyle — Thank you to the two churches I've had the privilege of serving as pastor: First Baptist Church of Clayton, New Mexico and First Baptist Church of Alamogordo, New Mexico. You have taught (and continue to teach me) how to shepherd. Thanks for the patience!

INTRODUCTION

He could've been born anywhere, at any time. Surely it would've made sense for the Savior of the world to be born in a major metropolitan hub, right? I mean, just imagine what kind of ministry Jesus could've had if his base of operations had been centered in Rome. He would've had direct access to the very ends of the earth Himself! A business card with "Jesus Christ, 300 Caesar Ave., Rome" would have looked pretty impressive. It would have turned heads. Gained attention. An expert from the big city! That would make people listen, wouldn't it?

Or how about Jerusalem? It sure would have made sense for the Jewish Messiah to be raised in Jerusalem, wouldn't it? Jerusalem was like Jew-central. It was the place where the Temple was—the building that for hundreds of years signified God's presence with his people. It was the place where Jesus' great-great-great-great grandfathers David and Solomon reigned. Imagine that business card for a second: "Jesus Christ, 1 Menora Way, Jerusalem." Wow. Just think of the impact He could have had if he had been raised in the center of Jerusalem. But, of course, he wasn't.

Instead, Jesus Christ, the Savior of the world, the long-awaited Messiah, the Holy Promised One, was raised in ... Nazareth. Nazareth was a place that wasn't thought of much or thought much of, really. In John 1, when Philip tells his brother, Nathaniel, that he has found the promised Messiah, Nathaniel's response is to simply ask, "Can anything good from out of Nazareth?" Not exactly a town that turned heads.

Nazareth was a small, insignificant town. It's so insignificant, in fact, that some people have actually argued it may never have existed at all in Jesus' day. However, archaeologists have discovered a few records referring to a place called Nazareth that predates even the Roman Empire. Apologists argue that Nazareth was so insignificant that if an author were trying to fabricate the story of Jesus, Nazareth wouldn't have even been on their radar as a location for Jesus to grow up. It was too insignificant to be considered important enough for fiction.

And yet, strangely enough, Nazareth–population around 400–was the hometown of the most important person to ever live. Why would God, in His divine wisdom, choose to allow Jesus to be raised in the middle of nowhere? Could it be because God wants us to understand something about the places the world has forgotten? Could it be that some of the most important work in the kingdom of God happen in nowhere places?

This book is written for those of you serving God faithfully in places that will never make it onto a "fastest-growing" list. This is for those of you living in places where there are a lot more cattle than there are people. Both of us have spent the vast majority of our ministry in places just like yours.

So, let us encourage you: you're not alone. God loves churches in the middle of nowhere. He loves people in communities that will never see the "hot now" neon sign at Krispy Kreme or the despair of wanting Chick-Fil-A on Sunday because you cannot even get it Monday through Saturday! He loves those towns that, to most of us, are nothing more than a name on an interstate exit sign.

Why does He love them? He loves them because there are millions of people around our nation who live in communities just like yours. He loves them because each and every man, woman, and child represented in the number on the population sign of your community are made in the image of God and deeply loved by Him. He loves small, rural communities because that's where Jesus grew up.

Not only does God love rural places, but we believe God is still doing some of His most amazing work even 2,000 years later. If you take a drive through the small towns that dot the landscape along America's backroads, you'll almost always find a church. And, if you happen to drop in on one some Sunday morning, you'll likely encounter a group of people who have worshiped together for years and (for the most part) love each other deeply.

Churches need pastors. And, as it turns out, pastors usually need churches to serve as well. Our aim in this book is to plead with seminary students and pastors young and old alike: consider rural churches. Consider giving your life to serving the Lord in a place the rest of the world has left in the rear-view mirror. We think you just might be amazed at what God does in and through you when you do.

So buckle up and let's take this journey to see what God wants to do in reclaiming rural churches for His glory through your preaching, praying, passion, and perseverance. God has a plan to reclaim rural, and you are a part of it!

Chapter 1

RECONSIDERING RURAL

I (Kyle) remember the email well. I just sat and stared at the words for several minutes, trying to process what I was reading. "I sent your resume to FBC Clayton." I had a lot of thoughts running through my mind. Most of them went something like, "He sent it *where*?" "Why? Why would he do that?"

I didn't have to look up Clayton, New Mexico on a map. I knew exactly where it was. My in-laws lived about 80 miles west of Clayton in an even smaller town called Springer. Every time we drove to their house, we went through Clayton. Their lone stoplight is where we would turn left. I knew exactly what was– or rather, *wasn't*–in Clayton. They were ninety miles from the closest Walmart. Wouldn't this be going backward?

When I got home that evening, I nonchalantly mentioned to my wife Michelle something about how my resume was sent to Clayton. I hoped she wasn't really paying attention. Maybe I could slip that part through. I still remember how she stopped and looked at me. Her reply was quick and to the point: "No."

Let me backup just a minute. At this point, I had served as a youth pastor in a few churches in West Texas over the prior seven years. Now I was feeling strongly the call to pastor. (One friend referred to it as "leaving the ministry to serve as a pastor.") I was serving in a small town that was about 15 miles from Abilene, TX. This was the closest we lived to civilization (aka, a city that had a Walmart) since we graduated from college seven years earlier. I had my eyes set on bigger cities–magical places like Dallas, San Antonio, or College Station. Places with Hobby Lobbies, Whataburgers, Starbucks, and Targets!

Over the course of about six months, I sent out a dozen or so resumes and waited for the calls to start flooding in. I had completed my Master of Divinity the previous year. I had several years' experience as a worship and youth pastor. I had been given the opportunity to preach in "big church" a few times and was armed with a couple of sermons on a CD that I readily handed out. I was headed for the big time. Except the calls didn't come. Slowly, I watched positions being filled without ever receiving a single phone call. I was starting to get desperate.

Now, allow me to take this moment to say that, until this point, I never once considered sending a resume outside of Texas. I mean, c'mon...it is *Texas* after all. I was finally–for the first time in my life–able to make a day trip to watch my beloved Texas Rangers play. I was born and raised in Texas. Texas was God's county. Matt likes to call it the "Great Republic." I knew a couple of college classmates who, for reasons I couldn't fathom, had left the great state for what I could only assume were third-world conditions in places like Florida and North Carolina (no offense, y'all). But that wasn't me. I married a New Mexico girl and got her to the Promised Land as fast as possible.

Both of our kids were born in Texas. Places like New Mexico and Hawaii were fun to visit for gorgeous scenery and delicious food, but Texas was home and always would be.

Except no churches in Texas were calling. So, in an act of desperation (probably on a Monday morning) and to at least say I'd tried everything, I contacted a buddy at the Baptist Convention of New Mexico (BCNM) and asked if there were any churches looking for a pastor in the state. He replied with a list of about thirty. Some were places I'd heard of like Albuquerque and Las Cruces; some were places I hadn't like Reserve and Lindrith. But, I had my mind set on a city. So, I sent my resume to my buddy, who passed it along to Dr. Joseph Bunce, the Executive Director of the BCNM.

After a phone call with Dr. Bunce discussing some of the churches in the state, I didn't hear anything for a month or so. Then came that email that would change my life: "I sent your resume to Clayton." After Michelle's initial response, I reminded her that we had resumes all over the place and we were sure to hear something from somewhere. "Don't worry, honey," I assured her. "We aren't moving to Clayton."

Fast-forward almost four years from that moment, and I found myself choking back tears as I announced to a congregation we had come to love that I had accepted a call to pastor First Baptist Church in Alamogordo, New Mexico. This place—Clayton, New Mexico—had become *home*. I had become their pastor. They had become *my* people—the people God had entrusted me with as an awfully green twenty-nine-year-old pastor. I had married some of them. I had conducted funerals for some of their parents and some of their children. As a volunteer firefighter, I fought a fire in one of our deacon's homes. This small town in the middle of nowhere had become home. And leaving it and the precious people there was harder than I could possibly have imagined four years earlier.

Here's what I've learned along the way: there are places just like Clayton, New Mexico all over the nation. They are places the rest of the world has forgotten about (it's called fly-over country for a reason, after all). But in these places are people who are serving God faithfully and who want to see the Kingdom of God expand in their communities and counties. And there are millions of men, women, and children who have never come to saving faith in Christ Jesus.

So, let us take these pages to try and convince you, with the Holy Spirit's help, why you should seriously consider packing up your family and moving to the middle of nowhere to serve the Savior in places that will never be graced by the green lady of Starbucks or the glorious golden arches of a McDonald's, and what you should do when you get there.

Rural Realities

According to the Southern Baptist Convention Annual Church Profile (ACP), a report that individual churches fill out and self-report to the SBC, there were 5,320,488 people gathered in a Southern Baptist church on any given Sunday in 2017. These folks gathered in 47,544 Southern Baptist churches. If you average that out, it comes to 112 people per church. Stop and consider that for a second. In the SBC, we have churches that will see tens of thousands of people come through their doors each and every week. We also have churches that see less than ten people in weekly worship attendance. But, if you run the figures, you wind up with 112 people gathered together in the average Southern Baptist church.[1]

Mark Clifton, the director of Replant for the North American Mission Board, likes to say that if you took all the pastors who serve churches that average less than 250 people in attendance on any given Sunday, you could fill a Major League Baseball stadium with them. Around 45,000 of the 47,000-plus churches in the SBC fall into that category. On the other end of the spectrum, he says you can fit all the pastors who serve SBC churches that average more than 1,000 in attendance on any given Sunday in a single jumbo jet: 250 people.

Mark has even shifted the language we use to identify churches under 250 in attendance. He doesn't call them small anymore. He now calls them "normative." If you have over 90% of the churches in a single denomination that share a single characteristic, you can call that normal. Churches that average under 250 in worship aren't small; they're normative.

Why does this matter? It matters because, with very few exceptions, in a rural setting you will be serving a normative-size church. In some cases, 250 people might rival the number of people who live in your community. In extreme cases, like Matt's church in Mayhill, New Mexico, the church will often run three times the population of the community in worship attendance!

If you go into a rural community with the expectation that you're going to run five-hundred in Sunday morning worship attendance in three years, you will probably be sorely mistaken. So, it's important to have realistic expectations when you arrive.

In this book we would like to offer four important keys to reclaim rural churches. No, these aren't exhaustive (and they aren't original to us), but we do believe them to be the foundation of an effective rural revitalization effort.

Chapter 2

PREACHING IN A RURAL CHURCH

Over the next few chapters, we will be considering the four p's in reclaiming rural churches; preaching, praying, passion, and persevering. While there could certainly be more layers to rural revitalization ministry, we believe these to be the foundation. In fact, without a headstrong focus on each, you will be setting yourself up for failure.

The first "p" is preaching. You are entering or continuing your ministry in a church with history. The pulpit you stand behind each Sunday has been the launching point, week in and week out, for the proclamation of the Word of God. In my (Matt) current church, there have been close to 12,000 sermons preached. Now let's be honest. There were some great ones and some not so great ones. Maybe your church has suffered through a dry spell for a few years from the pulpit and is in the spot it is in because the preaching of the Word has been neglected for a season.

That stops now.

The future health and vitality of your church depend wholly on a move of the Holy Spirit. We believe a large part of that will depend on your faithfulness to preach the Word. Paul charged Timothy, "Preach the word; be ready in season and out of season; rebuke, correct, and encourage with great patience and teaching," in 2 Timothy 4:2. And trust us, there will be seasons when you do not want to, and you would rather call in sick than suffer from another sermon where it feels like you are talking to a brick wall.

In fact, because of those dog days of preaching, you will be tempted to mail it in and reheat an old message, or simply focus on the felt needs of your church. Resist this temptation, brothers. Stake your ministry on the inerrant, infallible, and inspired Word of God. Listen: You are not inerrant. Your sermon is not infallible. But you are entering the pulpit with a Word that is not only inerrant and infallible but inspired by God. It's breathed out by God, "and is profitable for teaching, for rebuking, for correcting, for training in righteousness, so that the man of God may be complete, equipped for every good work," according to 2 Timothy 3:16-17. Preach the Word, preacher.

In 1989, seven words were whispered in a classic movie, Field of Dreams, "If you build it, they will come." While we have not been pastors for the entire 30 years since that classic hit the theaters, we have seen something similar over a combined 30-plus years of ministry: **"If you preach the Word, they will come."**

We both saw this mentality in student ministry, I (Matt) saw it also as a children's minister, and we continue to see it as teaching pastors. "If you preach the Word, they will come." We believe there is biblical reasoning for this, of course. In Acts 2, there is an incredible dynamic unfolding as they devoted themselves to the apostles teaching and fellowship, finding in verse 47, "Every day the Lord added to their number those who were being saved."

Granted, 20 or 30 years later we read Paul foretell in 2 Timothy 4:3–4, "For the time will come when people will not tolerate sound doctrine, but according to their own desires, will multiply teachers for themselves because they have an itch to hear what they want to hear. They will turn away from hearing the truth and will turn aside to myths." Nevertheless, the words preceding this warning to Timothy could not be clearer: "Preach the word" (2 Tim 4:2).

Biblical preaching may not always be popular. In fact, it may even cause you to lose some folks. However, the point is to be faithful. Neither one of us is all that smart or creative, but we have aimed for faithfulness, and God has blessed our efforts. Biblical preaching takes time, and you may have to look for it in every nook and cranny of your schedule, but it is absolutely necessary. After all, when Jesus said, "feed my sheep," we do not believe it was a suggestion—it was a command.

You may not have a "Field of Dreams" moment at your church, but you do have a responsibility to preach the Word. We have found, time and time again, they will come. Maybe not in droves, maybe not at great cost to you and your family, but we believe that may just be the reason for three more words in 2 Timothy 4:2, "with great patience."

"Rome wasn't built in a day," they say, and Jesus does not expect you to hit a home run each Sunday; He expects you to preach the Word. Your people do not need you to be the next

Dr. Adrian Rogers; they need (insert your name here) to preach the Word. Your patience and faithfulness in teaching may not get you to the conference circuit or on a platform to write books, and that is just fine. In fact, that might be a blessing. You simply need to preach the Word.

There are countless ways to "grow" the church you serve. You can build a full-size basketball court in the sanctuary or give away a car. You can chase after whatever the latest gimmick becomes. But there is only one "church-growth strategy" that will last — a church built on an everlasting foundation: the Lord and His Word. Fads will come and go, trends will shift by the seasons, but there is only one never-changing truth worth staking your church's future upon: the Lord and His Word.

You know what Jesus says in His parable on the two foundations in Matthew 7:24-27,

> Therefore, everyone who hears these words of mine and acts on them will be like a wise man who built his house on the rock. The rain fell, the rivers rose, and the winds blew and pounded that house. Yet it didn't collapse, because its foundation was on the rock. But everyone who hears these words of mine and doesn't act on them will be like a foolish man who built his house on the sand. The rain fell, the rivers rose, the winds blew and pounded that house, and it collapsed. It collapsed with a great crash.

You know what Jesus said to Peter in Matthew 16:18,

> I also say to you that you are Peter, and on this rock I will build My church, and the forces of Hades will not overpower it.

You know what Paul said to the Corinthians in 1 Corinthians 3:11,

> For no one can lay any other foundation than what has been laid down. That foundation is Jesus Christ.

Pastor, it is not your job to build your church. It is Jesus' job, and there is no foundation other than Him. If you will put your fruitfulness on the altar—along with your desires to grow a platform or build a name for yourself—and follow Paul's encouragement to Timothy to "preach the Word...with great patience," we believe Jesus will take care of the rest.

Perhaps it will be fast, perhaps it will be slow, and perhaps it will not even be that noticeable. However, over time, as you continue to preach the Word, they will come. And as they do, your members will grow and mature with each hit that advances the base runners. Stay faithful, stay patient, and preach the Word.

I (Matt) have been called to pastor two different churches that were plateaued and declining for years, and the temptation to get fancy and creative was strong, but I committed to faithful plodding, leaving the results to Him. I have entered the pulpit week in and week out and made my way through books of the Bible, verse by verse, and left the results up to Him. I was not that creative and I was not that imaginative, but I do believe I was faithful. One went from 30 or so to over 100; another went from around the same to as many as 172. In both, the Lord continued to keep the baptism waters flowing as the Spirit worked in, through, and perhaps even in spite of my sermons.

In other words, it was not built on my personality or abilities, but on the inerrant, infallible, and inspired Word of God. I trusted my faithfulness to preach the Word into the far more capable hands of Jesus and watched Him continue to build His church.

As you embark on or continue this journey of rural revitalization, do not neglect this. While you will need to be involved in your church members' lives throughout the week, on Sunday, they will gather. They will gather having experienced the ever-changing, overwhelming whims of society. Will they hear the never changing Word of God?

We charge you, right here, right now, to make a firm commitment to faithfully preaching the Word. There will be times you do not want to, times you want to "mail it in," but we beg you to keep your hand to the plow. Stick to the Bible, preach the unchanging Word, and watch the Spirit do His work.

Practical Points for
Preaching in a Rural Church

1. Get up early. In a rural church, the likelihood you may have to jump in the car in a moment's notice to go to the hospital that is an hour or more away is high. While you are there, your wife may even need you to go ahead and grab some milk on the way home because you will pass by that beacon of hope known as Walmart. While it is absolutely worth it, especially as the pastor of your people, it will make deep cuts into your sermon prep time. Get up early, grab your Bible, and get to work.

2. Read your passage a million times. Okay, that may be a bit of an exaggeration, but you might be reading this as a bi-vocational pastor—you may not have time to write out a 4,000-word manuscript, nor even need to. Read your text, know your text frontward and backward, and sketch out a healthy outline. If the week gets away from you, you will at least enter the pulpit and lean far more heavily on His Word and a simple, easy-to-follow outline than your ideas and pontifications. Come to think of it, that is the point!

3. Know your context and know your people. I (Matt) preached a revival in Kentucky during their undefeated run to the Final Four in 2015. I had been in Texas most of my life and had what I thought was a MONEY illustration involving football. However, as people started entering the sanctuary, I noticed several Kentucky basketball shirts. I did not know much about basketball, but I knew enough to shift my illustration on the fly to connect even more with the congregation. It was, forgive me, I'm gonna say it: a slam dunk. If you know your context and people well, you can be a city boy and still connect with people who think a traffic jam is when their cows are coming in to feed.

4. Books are your friend and so (sometimes) is the Internet. Your church likely will not provide you with a book budget and money might be tight. However, when you are able, grab a book on preaching and read it when you have some downtime. Also, many seminaries have blogs like Southwestern's Preaching Source, which offer sermon outlines and articles to help you in (and out of) the pulpit.

Chapter 3

PRAYING IN A RURAL CHURCH

Jesus' disciples heard all kinds of Jesus' teaching. They heard him teach for three years on the kingdom of God. They saw him raise the dead and heal the sick and crippled. They witnessed him walk on water and saw him feed thousands of people. With all of this flurry of activity over the course of three years, you'd think the disciples were really curious about all that Jesus taught them. They must have had a million questions. There were certainly things they just simply didn't understand.

And yet, the gospel writers only tell us one thing the disciples specifically asked Jesus to teach them. Luke 11:1 says, "He was praying in a certain place, and when he finished, one of his disciples said to him, 'Lord, teach us to pray, just as John also taught his disciples.'" Notice that the disciples did not ask Jesus to teach them to take up a love offering. They didn't ask him to teach them to gather a crowd. They didn't even ask him to pass on the power to multiply loaves and fishes. They wanted to learn to pray like Jesus prayed.

In the passage that follows, Jesus gives what we now know as the Lord's Prayer. It's become a standard prayer of liturgies and locker rooms. Catholics and county commissioners. Preachers and politicians. And yet, I'm not sure Jesus ever really intended the words of this prayer to serve as a kind of magic formula for reciting together before feasts or football games. Rather, I think he meant it as a simple model for bringing our needs before our loving Heavenly Father.

One of the keys to revitalization in any context is prayer. You have no power to revitalize anything on your own, nevermind the ability to see God's glory reclaimed in a church in the middle of nowhere. If you want to see God's kingdom expand in places that the world has passed by and passed over, it will require a reliance on the supernatural provision of God.

In this chapter, we will walk through the principles of the Lord's Prayer and how to apply them in our lives and ministry. So, grab your Bibles and follow along with us

Father, your name be honored as holy, v. 2a.

Rural church revitalization is all about seeing God's name being proclaimed in out-of-the-way places. This is where it starts. Ultimately, the goal of seeing churches revitalized is not simply to increase Sunday morning attendance or offering totals. It's not even about increasing the number of baptisms, as great as that may be. The goal of church revitalization is to make the name of God great in places where it has become an afterthought, if it's even a thought at all.

One of your daily prayers for the people in your church and community must be that they will come to honor the name of

God as holy. We want men and women, boys and girls to revere the name of Almighty God. We want to see people come to understand that Almighty God, the creator and sustainer of the Universe, is their only hope in this life and the life to come. Without this component, anything else we may accomplish in church revitalization is for naught. Unless we get this right, nothing else matters. Unless we understand this, we will miss the next part of this, too.

Your kingdom come, v. 2b.

As a church revitalization pastor, there is a concept you must learn: your church is not ultimate. God's plan to save the world is the Church. It includes your local church, but the kingdom of God does not depend on your church. Now, with that being said, the local churches you and I serve can play key parts in seeing God's kingdom come on the earth.

Your church is a part of God's strategic plan to reach your community for the kingdom of God. But hear this: you are (probably) not alone in this endeavor. In rural communities we cannot afford to be territorial. Often times you will have church members who split time between your church and another one in town. Perhaps you have members of your church who will supply preach at other churches in your association or network. It's not uncommon for churches in rural communities to partner together for big programs such as Vacation Bible School or Fall Festivals. You may or may not see people begin attending your church because of these events (often you will not). And that's ok. The Kingdom of God will last forever; your local church will not. If we are serious about seeing the Kingdom of God expand in our communities, I believe he will honor that by taking care of our local churches. As you spend time in prayer for your people, pray that they would have a heart for the kingdom of God to expand.

Give us each day our daily bread, v. 3.

Can I let you in on a little secret about rural church revitalization? You are most likely not going to be rich. Many of you reading this may be working two or even three jobs to support your family. Churches in nowhere places don't usually tend to be rolling in the money. Churches in communities like Corona, NM or Tahoka, TX don't usually spend exorbitant amounts of money to build a roller coaster in their sanctuary or rent a baseball stadium for their Easter service.

In a rural area, you're going to have to rely on God's provision for your family. There will be some tough days for you. But there will be tough days for your people as well. We've pastored in areas where the local economy was driven by farming and ranching. We've had prayer meetings asking God to send rain, and we've held prayer meetings pleading with God to stop the rain. We've rejoiced when crops were abundant, and we've wept when crops were absent.

God promises to meet the needs of His people, but that doesn't mean that He meets them according to our timelines. You might experience God's blessing in your bank account, or you might experience it in a side of beef (or if you're super extra-blessed, in elk meat). But make no mistake, God will provide. Praying that God will give us each our daily bread will keep us relying on Him in the times when there is plenty to go around and in times when we are struggling to keep the lights on. Pray that you will come to trust God for his provision in your life, and that the people in your church will come to trust God's provision for your life as well.

Forgive us our sins, v. 4a.

Can I let you in on another secret? You are a sinner. The people you pastor are sinners. We stand united with the people we serve in the simple fact that we are sinners in need of a great Savior. Why is this realization so important? Because, unless you as a pastor come to grips with the depth of your own sinfulness, you will be increasingly frustrated with your own (and your peoples') lack of progress.

A key part of praying every day is to ask the Lord to reveal your own sinful thoughts. King David was acutely aware of his own sinfulness. In perhaps the most vivid example of personal repentance in the Bible, David prayed in Psalm 51, "Be gracious to me, God, according to your faithful love; according to your abundant compassion." David understood his own sinfulness, but he also understood the depth of God's grace and mercy. That is what drove him to pray this beautiful prayer of repentance. It should drive us to our knees in prayer, repenting of sin, and praising God for his unending patience and forgiveness toward us.

For we also forgive everyone in debt to us, v. 4b

I just reminded you that you are, in fact, a sinner. That's important to remember, because the people whom you serve as pastor are also sinners. There will be times they act like sinners. Unless you first have a grasp on the forgiveness that God has shown to you, you will have a difficult time passing that forgiveness on to others.

As you come into a church revitalization, you will likely be leading some people who don't really want to be led. They may push back on some changes you feel are necessary. Some may even do more gossiping about you than talking to you about their concerns. If you are going to survive for any length of time, you will have to learn to be patient with them. Sanctification, like revitalization, is a long process. You must learn to be quick to forgive and slow to become angry when your people sin against you. You must be patient when they don't respond as quickly as you'd like.

Again, in this area, prayer is absolutely essential. You must constantly be in prayer for your people, particularly your critics, praying that God will do what He and He alone can do: Change their hearts. Just as you must be quick to repent of sins in your own life, pray that the people you shepherd would be quick to do the same.

Do not bring us into temptation, v. 4c.

Remember, pastor, you are a sinner. This means you will be prone to temptation. In the past couple of years, we have watched several high-profile leaders lose their ministries and, in some cases, their families because of moral failures. Satan loves to see leaders fall because of their sin.

Brothers, we cannot stress this point enough: You are not infallible. You are prone to mistakes. As the great musician Rich

Mullins sang, "We are not as strong as we think we are." At the moment you begin thinking you are beyond moral failure as a pastor, you just might be at your weakest.

Paul exhorted Timothy, "flee youthful passions and pursue righteousness, faith, love and peace" (2 Tim. 2:22). The traps of ministry are abundant, and none of us is immune to them. Be quick to repent of sins, asking forgiveness from God and those you may have wronged. Meet regularly with fellow pastors with whom you can pray and hold one another accountable as men of God.

Keep in mind that Paul called Timothy to set an example for the believers in his speech, conduct, faith, love and in purity. Pastor, pray that God will help you to remain faithful to Him in the middle of the temptations that come in this life.

A Prayerful Pastor

"Pray continually." These words in 1 Thessalonians 5:17 remind us that praying is to be a constant reality for believers. This is certainly true for pastors as well. If you want to serve your church well as pastor, you must be a man of prayer. That doesn't mean that you have to spend hours with your head bowed and eyes closed. It does mean you will spend a lot of time conversing with God's people and conversing with God about His people.

If you're already serving in a rural context, you have probably realized that you will spend quite a bit of time behind a steering wheel. It's likely that you have people who live a long way from your church. They drive a long way to go to the hospital or to go to Wal-Mart. When I (Kyle) pastored in Clayton, New Mexico for 3 ½ years, many of our church members' primary hospital was in Amarillo, TX, which was 2 hours away. Often, I would make that drive just to spend 15 or 20 minutes with a church member in their hospital room or to pray with them before a surgery. A long drive provides a lot of opportunity to spend in prayer for yourself, your family, and your people.

Finally, don't underestimate the power of a simple phone call, text message, handwritten note or email telling your folks that you are praying for them. One of the most encouraging parts of my week is a text message I receive from a church member that simply says, "I'm praying for you today." It comes at different points each week, but it often comes at just the moment that I need to know that someone is praying for me. Trust the Lord's guidance and, when he prompts, spend a few moments in prayer for your congregants and let them know you're praying for them.

Practical Points for
Praying in a Rural Church

1. Pray through your membership list. Make this a priority early in your ministry. Get an updated list of church members and regular attenders. Pastor Brian Croft recommends systematically praying through your church membership list at least once a month. If you're in a normative size church, this should be easily doable. Then, let your folks know that you're praying for them. Send them a note, a text message, an email, call them ... do *something* to let them know that you're praying for them often.

2. Gather for prayer often. Certainly, there should be prayer in your weekly worship service and in your small groups and other Bible studies. But what would it look like to simply gather together once a month for no other purpose than to pray? You might only have a couple of people show up at this meeting, but that's ok. Spend time praying for your church. At our monthly prayer gathering on the first Sunday evening of the month, we pray through a passage of Scripture, then we canvas our sanctuary in prayer. We pray for the spots where we know people usually sit, and we pray for the spot where we know no one usually sits. Often there are only three or four of us. But we've made this a priority to gather for no other purpose than to pray.

3. Pray through Scripture. Dr. Donald Whitney has written a phenomenal little book called *Praying the Bible*[2]. We highly recommend it to you as a way to systematically spend time in personal prayer with God's Word.

4. Seek ways to incorporate meaningful prayer into your worship service. If the only time you pray in your service is as a "transition," you are communicating something about prayer.

In our service, we pray for missionaries during our announcement time, we pray at the end of the musical worship, we pray after I read the main text for the sermon, we pray at the end of the sermon, we pray before we take the offering, and we pray after the offering has been received. Take a look at your worship service outline and see how you can pray more purposefully.

Chapter 4

PASSION IN A RURAL CHURCH

I (Matt) remember it like it was yesterday. "I don't know that you'll like it here, brother," a member of the search committee said, "there's not much to do, you might be bored." Underneath my polite smile was two eyes rolling and the reminder I have four daughters–there's no such thing as bored.

But let's be honest, it was a town of 57 people in the absolute middle of nowhere. Though we did have a café, we had a convenience store plastered with racist epitaphs and were nearly an hour away from the nearest Walmart. There really wasn't much to do.

Except win some souls for Jesus, I guess!

While I wholeheartedly believe it was a supernatural work of the Holy Spirit breathing life into that church, one thing He did was breathe life into me. He gave me a passion for a town that would otherwise be forgotten. I couldn't wait to get started, to get my boots on the ground, and to see what God was going to do.

One of the first decisions was dropped into my lap, choosing whether or not to continue Sunday night services. "There are just a handful of folks that come, if you want to end it, I'm sure it'll be fine," they said. My first thought was, "YES! Let's cut that out, and I can enjoy a longer Sunday afternoon nap!"

However, as I thought about it more and more, I realized a few things. First, those that were coming were mostly the backbone of our church. Second, I needed all the practice I could get in the pulpit. Third, while there's no Biblical reason to have two services, I thought there wasn't necessarily a reason not to.

I shared the passion I had with the folks, the excitement I had preaching the Word, and stressed the more informal nature of the time we could have on Sunday nights. I put in just as much study and prayer into those sermons and trusted Jesus to work in, through, and in spite of them. I asked the Spirit to grow within me a passion for "the few, the proud, the Sunday night crowd."

And He did.

I didn't badger people to come on Sunday night. In fact, I didn't do much more than let people know we would have church that night and what text we'd be studying. However, the passion the Spirit gave me began to infect the few that had been gathering. The few eventually became the many as we used our evening worship gatherings to study the Word a bit more informally, but no less passionately.

Brothers, what a privilege it is to pastor the bride of Christ! You've been entrusted with Jesus' sheep. That means you might get dirty and there'll be days that you will want to hang up the shepherd's staff and sell cars, but man. What a privilege!

Would you take a moment–right now–to thank God for the church He has given you or the church He may one day give you? Consider what a great responsibility that is! I believe this will help our outlook shift from pastoring them as a chore into joy, and passion will be the byproduct.

Keep your eyes on Jesus, who, as Hebrews 12:2 says, "For the joy that lay before him, he endured the cross, despising the shame, and sat down at the right hand of the throne of God." For the joy that lay before him, Jesus endured the greatest agony imaginable. Let me be clear: you can handle a couple of bad days. Not only that, you can do so with a little pep in your step. I mean, think about it…

You preach the Word of God to the people of God in the house of God indwelt by the Spirit of God; I can't think of a better reason to have a little passion! Whether you're preaching to 5 or 50, do so with passion! Over time, it will begin to infect the members of your church.

Now, it's easy to have some passion while preaching, but what about the other stuff we have to do? Paul says in Colossians 3:23-24, "Whatever you do, do it from the heart, as something done for the Lord and not for people, knowing that you will receive the reward of an inheritance from the Lord. You serve the Lord Christ."

You might have to clean some toilets or visit sister Claire after her bunion surgery. You might have to endure a contentious business meeting after you changed what room the quilt club met in, or even have to help a member corral a stray cow.

But do it from the heart, do it for the Lord–do it with passion, do it because you love them. It won't be glamorous. I mean, what did you expect from a book with the word "rural" in the title? But it's worth it because there's a reward at the end of this cornfield with a reminder from Paul: "You serve the Lord Christ."

Scan back up and reread those five words. Memorize it and remind yourself of it often. Remember them when it seems like you're stuck in mud (figuratively or literally), as you don't see the progress you expected. "You serve the Lord Christ."

The same Christ who endured the cross for you to reconcile you to a holy and righteous God...for the joy that lay before him. You serve him by serving the sheep He came to save...for the joy that lay before you; "an inheritance from the Lord." Do you love them enough to serve them? As you serve them, you serve Jesus. As you love them, you love Jesus.

One of my (Matt) best memories at Mayhill Baptist was going "shed hunting" with one of our members. Each year, the elk that easily outnumber the people in our town "shed" their antlers and it is a rather lucrative business, scouring the various mountains in search of them. For us, however, it was a chance to hike. It was a chance to get to know one another. We talked about marriage, we talked about our hobbies, we talked about Jesus, and we talked about Whataburger and how much I missed it. More importantly, we were simply together–out in the middle of nowhere, while I desperately tried not to freak out as we climbed up and down dangerous mountains.

I could have easily used that time in the study or reading a book, but it was time well spent. My love for him, the shared love we had for our Savior, and bond we shared as brothers in

Christ formed a friendship we would have otherwise missed had I chosen to spend the day in my study instead of searching for antlers hidden among various things that wanted to cut or bite me knowing full-well I was a city boy. We had nothing in common; he had just gotten out of the army, I had just gotten out of seminary; he had muscles, I...didn't; he came carrying enough supplies to withstand the apocalypse, I came with a bottle of water and a bag of trailmix. There was nothing to connect us other than a mutual love for Christ.

I have also been known to spend time with folks as they feed cattle or ride horses. And trust me, it is not because I like cattle or horses. In fact, I am rather uncomfortable around things that could easily send me to heaven in one fell swoop. However, my love for my people means there are instances when my time is better spent on a ranch than my study. It is one thing for your people to know you love the Lord and you love His Word, but do they know you love them? They will as you spend time with them!

Be willing to look a little silly if it means your people will get to know you outside the four walls of the church or behind the pulpit. We have considered the necessity of preaching and praying, but now we implore you to also show your people you do not only have a passion for the Word, you have passion for them. Get out of your study and into their lives.

Practical Points for
Passion in a Rural Church

1. Birthdays, y'all. Curate a list of the birthdays of each of your members and write them a handwritten note or give them a call on their birthday. Many will go to the mailbox each day and get ready to toss the latest spam they received. But a letter from you? They will cherish it!

2. Widows and widowers. On holidays like Thanksgiving or Christmas, and certainly Valentine's Day, make it a point to contact the widows and widowers in your church. Many are lonely, many of them missed the loved ones that have gone before them. Do not forget them around important holidays. Instead, make them feel special. Give them a call, invite them over for dinner, or go by and visit them.

3. Smile! I joke that I have resting Baptist face, but it is true. I actually write in my notes here and there to remember to smile. I love to preach the Word, but sometimes, my face fails to show it. Preach with passion, brothers! Do not put on a show, but do your church a favor and at least look like you are enjoying the absolute privilege you have to proclaim the Word.

4. Mingle, mingle, mingle. We get it. Your mind it set on the Word you are about the preach, but the time before and after the service is a great time for you to mingle with the people you serve. So, get out there and mingle! Ask how they are doing and, get this–this is earth-shattering–actually listen to them!

Chapter 5

PERSEVERING IN A RURAL CHURCH

We come to this final "p" in reclaiming rural churches after considering the necessity of preaching, praying, and passion, with a call for perseverance. In some ways, this is not reinventing the wheel, but reiterating the call to preach, pray, love, and stay we hear in many replanting and revitalization circles. However, they need to be repeated because we far too often forget. We quit too soon.

Jim-Bob got angry the special music on Memorial Day did not include the military service songs, and you were not wearing your American flag tie. Sue-Anne puts you on blast on Facebook because you preached two minutes past noon. Your budget has been in the red so long, John Hagee could write a book about it. You reach for the rip-cord, and off you go, you are out of there!

Ministry is hard, that is a given, and we have never experienced something as hard as rural church ministry. I (Matt) have served in the inner city and suburban contexts, which had their difficulties, but nothing compares to being in the middle of nowhere, ten miles out of cell range, and the morning conversations between the elk and turkey that provide the soundtrack for my mountain life.

When you are a bit more isolated, and on your own, it seems to be harder to get out of your slumps. The closest pastor to you might be 30 or more minutes away, and the deer in your front yard do not seem to be able to wrap their mind around what you are going through. It is in those seasons when the difficulties you face can make you search for your exit ramp far too soon, and often, just before a breakthrough.

Resist it, brothers. Lay down your roots and persevere. There will be some phenomenal days of ministry, there will be days when you just cannot seem to win, and everything in between. But if you aim to revitalize or replant a church, you need to realize you just signed up to climb Mt. Everest, backward while carrying 115 years of baggage on your back.

You will slip, you will fall, and you will likely face an avalanche of criticism along the way, but something is amazing about planting that flag on the top of the mountain because there is no way you can say, "Look what I did." No, that's a flag that says, "Look what God did!" After all, our "chief end," according to the London Baptist Confession of Faith (1689) is to "glorify God and enjoy Him forever."

So when Jim-Bob is chewing on you in your office, or you come across Sue-Anne's Facebook gripe, remember what James says in James 1:12, "Blessed is the one who endures trials, because when he has stood the test he will receive the crown of life that God has promised to those who love him." What a promise for us, brothers! The trials–big and small–are worth it!

And not only do our trials come with a promise for the future, but they also hold a purpose for the present. Paul says in Romans 5:3-5, "we also rejoice in our afflictions, because we know that affliction produces endurance, endurance produces proven character, and proven character produces hope. This hope will not disappoint us, because God's love has been poured out in our hearts through the Holy Spirit who was given to us."

So brothers, welcome those trials with open arms and persevere through them. When we quit too soon, we not only miss out on a potential blessing, but we also move our church even farther back. Instead, play the long game. Decide from the beginning that, barring a clear call from the Lord, you will be there indefinitely. Sign a blank check to the Lord for that church and tell Him, "Spend me as You will."

Now, it is one thing for you to decide from the beginning that you will not be a quitter the moment the going gets tough, it is another thing to serve in such a way as to not be run out of town with flaming torches and pitchforks. Lead and lead well, but remember to be patient.

Do not go in guns a'blazing because rural folk typically have guns, too. Spend the first few weeks and months getting to know your people—we mean really get to know them. Learn who they are, learn their names, find out what their story is, and find out about their hopes and dreams...and do not ever stop doing this! However, it is absolutely critical in the beginning.

As you do that, share with them your story and the hopes and dreams you have for your church. You might be surprised, some of the folks you get to know are already a few steps ahead of you and they may be the first ones in your corner because you took the time to get to know them. Also, a bit of a pro-tip here:

when possible, take your kids. Many of these folks are losing their health, their kids took their grandchildren away to the big city, and they are left with just about nothing but a needle, a thread, and the daily crossword puzzle. If you have kids, it will almost certainly bring an added measure of joy into their house they have not experienced in quite some time.

Along the way, keep your head on a swivel to take note of things that must be changed as soon as possible, things that need to be changed eventually, and just those things you would like to see happen one day. Make a list and patiently work your way through it as you go, one-by-one over time. In other words, you need to use what Mark Clifton calls, "tactical patience," which I like to relate as 'know when to hold them, know when to fold them.' You need wisdom to know which hills are worth dying on and then what can wait until you have some extra credibility under your belt. After all, James 1:5 reminds us, "Now if any of you lacks wisdom, he should ask God—who gives to all generously and ungrudgingly—and it will be given to him."

One of the greatest helps we have discovered is the necessity of partnerships and friendships, especially when trials come in wave after wave. While we have one another, we were both quick to reach out to pastors that had been in the area for several years (some even a couple decades) to learn, vent, and lean on in the early days of our ministries in rural New Mexico. We were also quick to plug into our local associations, which added yet another layer of help. There is no reason to go at it alone. Surround yourself with fellow co-laborers who will encourage you in both the good times and the bad, and help you persevere through them all.

Advice from Those in the Field

Ok, now that we've reached this point in this chapter, we have a confession to make. Neither of us has done this very well. We have not modeled persevering very well. As we speak, Kyle's longest-tenured position is 3 ½ years and Matt's is 3 years. While we have certainly learned some principles through the years that will, prayerfully, allow us to stick it out in our current pastorates, we wanted to let you hear from a couple of men who have persevered well in rural church settings. We've had the privilege of getting to know both of these men because they both serve in our local Baptist association in New Mexico. Chances are that you have not heard of either of these men (or either of these towns, for that matter). So, before we share with you the tips we learned from them, understand this: pastoring long-term in a rural setting will probably not lead to fame or fortune. Your name and church may never be mentioned among the "movers and shakers" of your denomination. But you just may see God do some big things in small places for the sake of his kingdom.

Hayden Smith is currently in his 30th year serving as pastor at First Baptist Church in Carrizozo, New Mexico. Cal West is serving in his 20th year as pastor at First Baptist Church in Corona, New Mexico. We were able to ask them both some questions about their experiences serving long-term in a rural setting. They provided some key insights.

Did you have plans to be in your church 20+ years when you first arrived?

Cal explained that he moved to Corona, NM to work on a ranch, thinking his pastoring days were over. He became the interim pastor in 1999 then accepted the call to become pastor in January 2000.

Hayden moved to Carrizozo, NM in 1989. He explained that he once attended a church where the pastor served for ten years and who taught him that pastors (and laymen, for that matter) should be where God wants us. He said this pastor explained that people often climb the "ladder of success" only to find that the ladder was leaning against the wrong wall. He said he, his wife Cheryl, and the church were all in agreement that God should be in charge and that they were staying put until God revealed otherwise.

What is the hardest thing about being in a church long-term?

Hayden said the hardest part of pastoring long-term is that, over time, you grow really close to people. When they move or die, or go through difficult times, it hurts. They become like family. That means you get to see the good sides and bad sides of people and, sometimes, you come to know things you wish you din't know.

Cal said he couldn't think of any specific thing that has made it hard to serve long-term, but that he experienced some difficulties in recent years. "But then, I had some difficulties in churches where I pastored a shorter time." He said he averaged around three years prior to FBC Corona. In other words, pastoring can be difficult whether you're in a church short-term or long-term (hence the need for perseverance!).

What has been the biggest joy about being in a church long-term?

Cal said the biggest joy is getting to watch people grow in their faith. "Also, we've become a family. I've been privileged to watch kids grow from the womb to college and beyond."

Hayden said his biggest joy is seeing God work in the lives of people, even though that growth often happens slowly. He also said he appreciates the trust he has in the community at large because he has been in the community for so long.

What has made you stay put when it would have been really easy to move on?

Both men had the same response to this question: "God hasn't called me away." Cal said that God has given him a deep love for the flock with which he has been entrusted." Hayden reminded us that, ultimately, the churches we serve belong to God. He said there have been times when he's asked God if he should move, but God has never given any indication it was time to go.

How would you counsel a young pastor who's ready to call it quits and move on?

Both men had the same initial response to this question as well: "Pray!" Cal said, "I think I would tell them to pray earnestly to determine whether God was calling them away or if they were running away. Admittedly, there were times in the early years when I considered looking for greener pastures, but I'm so thankful I stayed." Hayden said something similar. "Every church has problems at some time or another. Are you running from a 'problem?'"

We'll close out this chapter with a quote we got from Hayden and, to be honest, it's difficult to think of a better illustration. Someone has said, "If you think the grass is greener on the other side of the fence, look for a septic tank. Those are probably leach lines."

Pastoring is hard. Pastoring in rural areas brings unique challenges. But the more we visit with pastors who have stuck it out long-term in one church, the more convinced we are that the blessings far outweigh the struggles of staying put. So, pastor, when it gets hard (and it will), hit your knees in prayer, then love your people well and remember that they are learning to love you well, too.

Practical Points for
Persevering in a Rural Church

1. Do not take criticism personally. You will inevitably make changes and there is a good chance these changes will upset a few folks. When they get upset, it will be easy to take it personally. If you do, you will develop a chip on your shoulder. With each criticism, you will gain another chip. Eventually, the burden will be too much and you will head for the nearest exit. While you should not ignore your critics, sift the criticism as best you can. Separate the constructive from the destructive; learn what you can from it and move on.

2. You cannot please everyone, though you will want to. We struggle to think of someone that lives to displease everyone; virtually everyone wants to be liked. But if you decide you would rather honor people's likes and dislikes than the Lord, your ministry will immediately be impotent. Instead, as Colossians 3:17 says, "whatever you do, in word or in deed, do everything in the name of the Lord Jesus, giving thanks to God the Father through him."

3. Rest. Both of us wear just about every hat there is to wear in our churches because it is necessary. However, it we do so without taking some breaks to refresh, we will wear out and burnout. Between the two of us, we get seven weeks off a year. You might get one or just a few. Whatever you get, take it. If you do not get it, ask for it, or carve out what you can during the week to turn off the phone and unplug. Working yourself into an early grave is not only stupid, it is sinful.

4. "Burn your ships." When Kyle became the pastor of First Baptist Alamogordo, he immediately bought a house because he knew he was going to be in an uphill battle. When I became the pastor of Mayhill Baptist, I immediately took my name off

every ministry job board I could remember. Neither one of us wanted an easy escape when times got hard—we were digging in and laying down some roots. If you have a resume on your computer and you have accepted a call to a church, delete it.

Chapter 6

THE CHURCH THAT THE WORLD FORGOT:

A Brief Look at Paul's Letter to the Colossians

At one point, Colossae was a major city. In fact, at the end of the fifth century, B.C., it was even described as a great city. But then things changed. Thanks to the conquering power of Alexander the Great, the flow of traffic changed and the city of Laodicea, 10 miles away, grew while the size and influence of Colossae waned. By the time Paul wrote his letter to the Colossian church, Colossae was no longer a big city. It was a small town that the world had, at best, bypassed and, even more likely, forgotten.

Maybe this sounds familiar. Perhaps when you drive down Main Street, there are far more storefronts closed and boarded up than there are open for business. Faded signs are a constant reminder of what the town once was. The morning conversations in the coffee shop often center around "the good ole' days" when the town was thriving. Perhaps a mayor or two have even run on a campaign promise to bring prosperity back to the community, only to be defeated four years later by another candidate promising the same thing but never delivering on the promise.

Yes, the world had forgotten all about Colossae. Perhaps the world has forgotten about your town as well. But rest assured, my fellow pastor, God has not forgotten. In the rest of this chapter, we will take a brief look at some highlights from Paul's letter to the Colossians. So grab your Bible, and let's walk through this short letter together.

Introduction and Thanksgiving (1:1-12)

Paul begins the letter to the church at Colossae by simply telling them he is thankful for them. "We always thank God, the Father of our Lord Jesus Christ, when we pray for you" (1:3). Paul wanted these precious people, "saints in Christ...who are faithful brothers and sisters," (1:2) to know that he cared for them and prayed for them often.

Paul then reminds them of the power of the gospel they proclaim. He told them that the gospel "is bearing fruit and growing all over the world, just as it has among you since the day you heard it and came to truly appreciate God's grace." The same gospel that Paul proclaimed to believers in Rome and to the religious leaders at the Areopagus in Athens is the gospel he reminded the Colossian believers of here. The gospel of Jesus Christ has power to save in New York City, and in the African bush, and in the cotton fields of West Texas. The gospel that Peter proclaimed on the day of Pentecost and saw 3,000 people saved is the same gospel that you declare to 20 people gathered in your sanctuary on Sunday morning. And it still has the power to save. Don't discount the power of the gospel.

The Glory of our God (1:13-23)

Paul goes on to remind his readers of the greatness of God and His immense grace shown to His people. "He has rescued us from the domain of darkness and transferred us into the kingdom of the Son he loves" (1:13). This is good news no matter where you are! Even if it feels like you've been exiled to the backside of nowhere, you are safe and secure in God's hand. Ultimately, this is the only thing that matters. While it can get awfully lonely when you're the only pastor for 45 miles, or when you and your wife may be the only couple in your church under the age of 60, rest assured that God has transferred you into His family! This is one of the keys to staying put with your hand to the plow of rural church ministry even on the hardest of days.

Then, in case the Colossian believers still weren't convinced of God's greatness, Paul reminds them of a hymn that was being recited by the early believers. "He is the image of the invisible God, the firstborn over all creation. For everything was created by him, in heaven and on earth, the visible and the invisible" (1:15-16). Paul reminded his readers that everything - things they could see and even things they couldn't see - were created by Almighty God. God still had a purpose for the city of Colossae, even if the residents weren't quite sure what that was. And He still has a purpose for your community as well. Even if that purpose is not abundantly clear to you at the moment, keep faithfully proclaiming His Word to His people, trusting that He is revealing His plans and purposes little by little.

Paul's Ministry to the Colossians (1:24-2:3)

It's likely that Paul has not yet even visited the church at Colossae at the time of his writing. But he wanted them to know he was serving alongside them for the sake of the kingdom of God. Even as he is writing from prison, Paul assures them he is suffering *on their behalf* in order that the gospel may be proclaimed to those in the city.

As we've discussed before, often people in rural contexts think the world has forgotten them. In fact, when you interview in a rural church, it's not uncommon to hear, "We don't know why anyone would want to come way out here." Your folks need to hear that towns in the middle of nowhere matter to God, and that they matter to God's people. Paul wanted to encourage believers in the small town of Colossae, and I believe he would want these words to encourage believers in your town as well.

Struggles in the Church (2:4-23)

The church in Colossae was apparently dealing with rampant false teaching. Paul wanted to make sure the believers there had a firm grasp on the truth of the gospel. If you've spent very long in a rural church, you've probably learned that some weird ideas can work their way into churches and communities. You most likely have some folks who believe things that are, at best, not biblical and, at worst, straight-up heretical.

For rural churches today, Paul's words still ring true: "Be careful that no one takes you captive through philosophy and empty deceit based on human tradition, based on the elements of the world, rather than on Christ" (2:8). You will have to counter false teaching with the truth of God's Word. This can take on many forms, from preaching exegetically, spending much time in focused prayer for your people, and through gently shepherding folks one-on-one. But, you must remind the folks in your church that, ultimately, the truth of God's Word will stand when human wisdom fails.

Realities of the Christian Life (3:1-4:6)

Paul knew the Colossian believers would be dealing with the everyday ins and outs of life. He addresses how to walk as followers of Christ (3:1-10), how to welcome men and women from different cultural backgrounds (3:11), how to relate to other believers (3:12-15), how to worship Christ (3:16-17), how families should relate to one another (3:18-21), and how slaves and masters should work together (3:22-4:1). He closes this section by encouraging the believers to devote themselves to prayer and to welcome outsiders with love (4:2-6).

Read through that list again. That's a lot of things to cover in just over one chapter! Mark Clifton has said it is imperative for a successful church replanter or revitalizer to be a resourceful generalist. That is, often times a pastor in a church replant must serve as a general practitioner in spiritual things. In these verses alone, we see that a pastor could be helping people grow in their spiritual life, serving as a marriage and family counselor, helping employers and employees deal with workplace issues, seeking to build bridges between people from different cultural and racial backgrounds, leading worship gatherings, and building fellowship within the body of Christ. No seminary degree in the world can effectively train a pastor in all of these areas. Many of these are learned in the trenches of ministry.

In rural settings, you may be the closest thing to a professional counselor in your community. Your may be called upon to help straighten out a wayward teenager or an out of control spending habit. You may well be approached by a dear couple who don't understand their brand new neighbors from the Middle East. You might be approached to give your opinion on the establishment of a new liquor store by the local city council. You will certainly be asked to perform weddings and funerals for folks you've never met before. And that could all happen in your first month on the job!

The simple fact is, there are a lot of facets to ministry, and this is especially true in rural settings. You may well be the community's only pastor, which means you will have influence well beyond the doors of your church building. So, as you prepare for ministry in a rural setting (or as you continue ministering in a small community), you need to be a pastor who has some knowledge on a wide range of topics. This doesn't mean you need to be an expert, but it does mean that you need to read widely. You need to develop a strong network of pastors in other areas whom you can lean on and learn from.

Conclusion (4:7-18)

Take a couple of minutes and read through this passage… We'll wait…

What did you notice? In these 12 verses, Paul mentions 11 names. Paul did not minister alone. He had a large group of people who served alongside him, whether they were physically with him or not. The same needs to be true of you, fellow pastor. We cannot stress enough the importance of networking together. In our own denomination (the Southern Baptist Convention), we cooperate together with other churches in our area through the local association, with our state convention, and on the national level through the SBC. We have brothers in ministry whom we meet with regularly for times of prayer and encouragement. Many small towns have active ministerial alliances that will provide this avenue of fellowship and encouragement. In extreme rural settings, perhaps you could form a group who meets often through video chat to pray for and encourage one another.

The point is this: you need partners. We are convinced that brothers in ministry are essential to persevering in nowhere places for the glory of God. If you don't know where to start, we would encourage you to visit www.churchreplanters.com to get in touch with other pastors in similar contexts. You are not alone. There are pastors all across North America who are serving in churches just like yours who are probably looking for others to connect with as well.

God Cares for Communities that the World Forgot

From this short book of Colossians, we learn that God cares deeply for churches in communities that the rest of the world couldn't even locate on a map. He knows exactly where you are, and he loves the people in your community more than we could ever imagine. The gospel of Jesus Christ is powerful. It's powerful in major cities, in the fancy suburbs, and in the hundreds of small towns at the intersection of nowhere and forsaken.

We are convinced that some of the most powerful work of God happens in the lives of pastors and churches that will never win an award for most baptisms or highest giving in our denominations. We firmly believe that God loves pastors who serve in areas where the cattle or deer far outnumber the people. And we believe that God will be with you every step of the way as you serve His people in communities the rest of the world never even now exist.

NOTES

[1] Figures taken from http://www.sbc.net/BecomingSouthernBaptist/
pdf/FastFacts2018.pdf

[2] Whitney, Donald. *Praying the Bible.* Crossway: 2015.

It is time for
radical partnership.

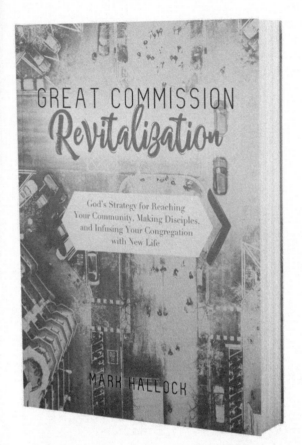

the
Replant
Series

This series features short, action-oriented resources aimed at equipping the North American church for a movement of church replanting, introduced by Pastor Mark Hallock's book *Replant Roadmap*.

Thousands of churches are closing their doors in United States every year in some of its fastest-growing, most under-reached neighborhoods. Yet there is much hope for these churches, particularly through the biblically-rooted, gospel-saturated work of replanting.

Designed for both group and individual study, these books will help you understand what the Bible has to say about how God builds and strengthens his church and offer you some practical steps toward revitalization in your own.

For more information, visit **acomapress.org** and **nonignorable.org**

ACOMA PRESS

Acoma Press exists to make Jesus non-ignorable by equipping and encouraging churches through gospel-centered resources.

Toward this end, each purchase of an Acoma Press resource serves to catalyze disciple-making and to equip leaders in God's Church. In fact, a portion of your purchase goes directly to funding planting and replanting efforts in North America and beyond. To see more of our current resources, visit us at *acomapress.org*.

Thank you.